DEPARTMENT OF THE NAVY
HEADQUARTERS UNITED STATES MARINE CORPS
2 NAVY ANNEX
WASHINGTON, DC 20380-1775

MARINE CORPS ADMINISTRATIVE PROCEDURES

DEPARTMENT OF THE NAVY
HEADQUARTERS UNITED STATES MARINE CORPS
2 NAVY ANNEX
WASHINGTON, DC 20380-1775

MCO 5000.14D
MI
4 Jun 04

MARINE CORPS ORDER 5000.14D

From: Commandant of the Marine Corps
To: Distribution List

Subj: MARINE CORPS ADMINISTRATIVE PROCEDURES (SHORT TITLE: MCAP)

Encl: (1) Key Administrative References
      (2) Individual Marines' Administrative Responsibilities
      (3) Commanders' Responsibilities for Personnel Administration
      (4) Responsibilities of G-1s, S-1s, and Administrative Officers
      (5) Installation Personnel Administration Centers
          Responsibilities
      (6) Responsibilities of the Manpower Information Systems Support
          Office

1. <u>Purpose</u>. This Order provides guidance concerning the function and organization of Marine Corps administration. The primary goal of this Order is to increase the quality of administrative support provided and to establish uniformity throughout all levels of administrative and personnel support. The enclosures provide details on the typical division of administrative responsibilities and functions between individuals, leaders, and the supporting staffs/organizations.

2. <u>Cancellation</u>. MCO P5000.14C.

3. <u>Background</u>

   a. One of the fundamental responsibilities incumbent upon Marine Corps leaders is ensuring the prompt, precise reporting and maintenance of the information that comprises the official records of the Marines under their charge. As accurate personnel information and effective administrative processes are key enablers of our ability to "take care of our Marines" and maintain a force capable of winning our Nation's battles, it is imperative that standard procedures be implemented where practical.

   b. In the early years, Marine Corps "personnel administration" consisted primarily of pay rosters maintained at the unit level. As the need for information and standard processes grew, administration evolved to capitalize on information technology systems that were fielded to support unit level administration. Although these systems provided tremendous increases in capability over previous methods, their complexity required personnel administrative functions be consolidated at the battalion level. To further capitalize on improvements in technology and to respond to a mandated reduction of administrators, consolidation above the battalion and squadron level was directed in 1999. However, as definitive guidance was not provided on how to conduct this consolidation, an environment was created where personnel administrative services are provided using varied methods across the Marine Corps, and commanders were forced to obligate local funds to build systems to bridge gaps in the administrative processes. While these consolidations did not diminish the leader's responsibility for the accuracy of their Marines information, in many cases the consolidation reduced a leader's access to personnel information and processes.

4. Goal. The goal of Marine Corps Administration is to provide commanders, Marines, and their family members effective administrative support and services. Enabling commanders to focus more resources on training and operations, and ultimately facilitating mission accomplishment, are inherent in this goal. Providing Marines and their family members with increased quality of life through efficient administrative support will also increase unit and individual readiness. Supporting considerations include:

a. Establishing the most effective use of personnel and equipment resources to accomplish administrative requirements, along with quality control and improve organizational structures that ultimately enable increased supervision, coordination, and integration.

b. Maintaining vigilance toward complete, accurate personnel records. This includes Official Military Personnel Files, paper Service Record Books and Officer Qualification Records, and electronic records including the Marine Corps Total Force System.

5. Types of Marine Corps administration. The four types of Marine Corps Administration are General, Operational, Manpower, and Personnel Administration.

a. General Administration. General administration encompasses those management functions that provide direct support to the commander. Typical general administrative tasks include preparation of correspondence and messages, oversight of the postal, career retention, and awards programs, the processing of personnel requests, the management of the Classified Material Control Center (CMCC) and Directives Control Point (DCP), and ensuring the accuracy and timely submission of all performance evaluations. General Administrative tasks are normally assigned to a G-1, S-1/Adjutant, or unit or section administrative officer.

b. Operational Administration. Operational Administration includes those administrative requirements that directly support the operational mission of the organization. Examples includes sourcing individual augmentations and combat replacements, reporting of personnel statistics to higher component and joint commands via the JPERSTAT, reporting and tracking of casualties, developing deployment manpower data, determining personnel estimates of supportability, and developing Annex E to Operations Plans and Operations Orders.

c. <u>Manpower Administration</u>. Manpower Administration includes the optimal allocation of human resources throughout the command or unit. These tasks include internal assignments, strength-reporting, managing and validating personnel security clearance requirements, and manpower process advisement.

d. <u>Personnel Administration</u>. Personnel Administration functions involve reporting and maintaining information that affects a Marine's pay, compensation, promotion, military readiness, personal readiness, and family readiness.

6. <u>Advocacy</u>

a. <u>Functional Advocacy</u>. The Deputy Commandant, Manpower and Reserve Affairs (DC, M&RA) is the Functional Advocate for Marine Corps Administration. As the Functional Advocate, the DC, M&RA is responsible for occupational field sponsorship, providing administrative guidance, policies, and orders, and the development and management of Marine Corps manpower and personnel information systems.

b. <u>MAGTF Advocacy</u>. The Deputy Commandant, Installations and Logistics (DC, I&L) is the Advocate for the Supporting Establishment. The administrative functions located at Installation Personnel Administration Centers (IPACs) will, by definition, be provided by the supporting establishment, therefore, the DC, I&L has a contributing role in Marine Corps Administration. The DC, I&L's responsibilities include assisting in the proper structuring of IPACs, coordinating the integration of IPAC functions with other supporting establishment capabilities, and planning for adequate facilities.

7. <u>Concepts and Responsibility</u>

a. Concepts. Administrative technical expertise will be consolidated at the highest possible organizational level commensurate with operational requirements. Information will be collected as close to the source as possible and reviewed, certified, and reported in systems of record with the minimum number of intermediate steps. Direct reporting by individuals and leaders will be facilitated whenever procedurally and technically possible. IPACs will be the standard configuration for Marine Corps consolidated administration and Marine Corps policies will be reviewed and rewritten to support this concept.

b. Responsibility. Nothing in this Order diminishes leaders' responsibilities for effective administration of their organizations, Marines, and their families. Rather, the IPAC supports commanders by relieving them of the burden of maintaining technical expertise of higher-level, frequently esoteric administrative functions. The OIC of the IPAC will maintain a viable and constant communication link with the special staff sections, and the unit(s) served to ensure proper administration. All must coordinate administrative actions and pursue the goal of providing the highest quality administrative support possible to Marines and commanders.

8. <u>Action</u>. This Order provides guidance to establish standardized Marine Corps personnel administrative support, by directing:

    a. A phased movement to IPACs located in the supporting establishment thereby relieving operational commands of selected support functions and permitting them to focus on their core mission requirements.

    b. The development of improved tools and processes that return to commanders, leaders, and Marines the proper balance of access to information, authority, and responsibility for reporting and maintaining personnel information. The first of these tools is the ongoing fielding of the Total Force Administration System (TFAS). TFAS will provide the foundation that enables the Marine Corps to effectively leverage emerging systems and concepts, and positions the Marine Corps for the eventual migration to the DoD mandated Defense Integrated Military Human Resources System.

    c. The review of the 01XX occupational field to determine the appropriate number of structure spaces to be transferred to the IPACs while leaving sufficient 01XX structure in the operating forces to provide required support. Additionally, as there is an ever-increasing requirement to return Marines to the operating forces this review will maximize the use of civilian Marines to perform administrative functions and determine the number of billets that can be made available to fill deficiencies in other military occupational speciliaties.

9. <u>Summary of Revision</u>. This Order has been reformatted and contains a substantial number of changes and must be reviewed in its entirety.

10. <u>Recommendations</u>. Recommendations concerning the contents of Marine Corps Administrative Procedures Order are invited, and should be forwarded the Commandant of the Marine Corps (MI).

11. <u>Reserve Applicability</u>. This Order is applicable to the Marine Corps Total Force.

GARRY L. PARKS
By direction

DISTRIBUTION: PCN 10207021000

    Copy to: 7000023 (25)
                7000260 (2)
                7000144/8145001 (1)

KEY ADMINISTRATIVE REFERENCES

Below is list of frequently used administrative references. This list is not all-inclusive. As regulations are frequently updated, users should verify with the source of the publication that they are using the current reference.

DoD 4525.8-M: DOD OFFICIAL MAIL MANUAL
Provides instructions for implementing the nine-digit ZIP Code System for Marine Corps Units.

DoDPM: DEPARTMENT OF DEFENSE MILITARY PAY AND ALLOWANCES ENTITLEMENT MANUAL
Provides statutory provisions for entitlements, deductions, and collections and establishes Department of Defense policy on the pay and allowances of military personnel.

DoDI 7000.14: DEPARTMENT OF DEFENSE FINANCIAL MANAGEMENT REGULATIONS – VOLUME 9, TRAVEL POLICY AND PROCEDURES
This volume provides supplemental instructions on the payment of allowances authorized by the JFTR/JTR. The policies and procedures addressed in this volume apply to all personnel traveling under orders funded by the Department of Defense. This includes military members, DoD civilian employees, members of the Reserve Components, family members on official orders, and travelers on DoD Invitational Travel Orders (ITOs).

FMFM 3-1: COMMAND AND STAFF ACTIONS (PCN: 13900014500)
Sets forth doctrine, procedures, and techniques for the execution of command and staff action within the Marine Corps.

JAGINST 5800.7: MANUAL OF THE JUDGE ADVOCATE GENERAL (JAGMAN)
(PCN: 40900580000)
Provides regulations and guidance for courts of inquiry, investigations, claims, etc., to include authority of Armed Services personnel to perform notaries acts.

MANUAL FOR COURTS-MARTIAL, UNITED STATES (PCN: 50100339000)
Contains the rules for courts-martial, the military rules of evidence, the punitive articles, and non-judicial punishment procedures as they apply to members of the military services.

MARINE CORPS MANUAL (PCN: 50100342500)
The Marine Corps Manual is designed primarily for use by Marine Corps commanders and their staffs. It contains such items as delegation of authority, inspections, directive requirements, etc. and should be used with U.S. Navy Regulations to ascertain departmental policy as it relates to the Marine Corps.

ENCLOSURE (1)

MCO P1000.6: ASSIGNMENT, CLASSIFICATION AND TRAVEL SYSTEMS MANUAL (ACTS MANUAL) (PCN: 10200010000)
Contains instructions, procedures, and regulations for classification and testing, distribution, assignment, and transfer of officers and enlisted personnel.

MCO P1001R.1: MARINE CORPS RESERVE ADMINISTRATIVE MANAGEMENT MANUAL (MCRAMM) (PCN: 10200030000)
Contains instructions for Marine Corps Reserve administrative and management policies.

MCO 1001.39: PRE-SEPARATION COUNSELING CONCERNING MARINE COPRS RESERVE (MCR) PARTICIPATION (PCN: 10200090000)
Provides counseling guidance and administrative instructions relative to qualified enlisted Marines who are being separated from active duty concerning participation in the Marine Corps Reserve.

MCO 1001.52: ACTIVE RESERVE (AR) SUPPORT TO THE RESERVE COMPONENT (RC) (PCN: 10200135900)
Prescribes policies and procedures pertaining to the selection, assignment, utilization, and administration of Marine Corps Reserve personnel who provide full-time, active duty support to the Reserve component within the Total Force Marine Corps.

MCO 1001R.54: MARINE CORPS RESERVE INCREMENTAL INITIAL ACTIVE DUTY FOR TRAINING (IIADT) PROGRAM (PCN: 10200136100)
Contains information and instructions for the administration of the IIADT Program in the Marine Corps Reserve.

MCO P1020.34: MARINE CORPS UNIFORM REGULATIONS (PCN: 10200150000)
Contains current policies regarding the wearing of Marine Corps clothing.

MCO 1040.43: ENLISTED-TO-OFFICER COMMISSIONING PROGRAM (PCN: 10200281400)
Sets forth the requirements and regulations whereby commanding officers may nominate qualified enlisted Marines (MCP) and enlisted Marines may apply for assignment to Officer Candidates School (ECP) and subsequent appointment to unrestricted commissioned officer grade in the U.S. Marine Corps Reserve.

MCO 1040.22: NAVAL FLIGHT OFFICER (NFO) PROGRAM (PCN: 10200240000)
Sets forth the provisions whereby active duty commissioned officers may submit applications for assignment to the NFO Program.

MCO P1040.31: CAREER PLANNING AND DEVELOPMENT GUIDE (PCN: 10200280200)
Contains policies and procedures to be used in the conduct of the Marine Corps Career Planning Program.

ENCLOSURE (1)

MCO P1040R.35: MARINE CORPS RESERVE CAREER PLANNING GUIDE
(PCN: 10200280600)
Contains policies and procedures to be used in the conduct of the Marine Corps Reserve Career Planning Program.

MCO P1050.3: REGULATIONS FOR LEAVE, LIBERTY, AND ADMINISTRATIVE ABSENCE
(PCN: 10200310000)
Provides regulations and policies on leave, liberty, and administrative absence.

MCO P1070.12: MARINE CORPS INDIVIDUAL RECORDS ADMINISTRATION MANUAL (IRAM) (PCN: 10200430500)
Provides policies, procedures, and technical instructions for the administration of personnel records.

MCO P1080.20: MARINE CORPS TOTAL FORCE SYSTEM CODES MANUAL (MCTFSCODESMAN) (PCN: 10200470000)
Contains information used in connection with personnel reporting matters in MCTFS

MCO P1080.40: MARINE CORPS TOTAL FORCE SYSTEM PERSONNEL REPORTING INSTRUCTIONS MANUAL (MCTFSPRIM) (PCN: 10200571000)
Provides policies, procedures, and technical instructions regarding the reporting of personnel information into the MCTFS.

MCO 1130.53: ENLISTMENT INCENTIVE PROGRAMS (PCN: 10200690000)
Provides instructions for the administration of the Enlistment Bonus Program.

MCO P1200.7: MILITARY OCCUPATIONAL SPECIALTIES MANUAL (MOS MANUAL)
(PCN: 10200760000)
Presents the job structure and career development structure which enables the Marine Corps to carry out its assigned mission.

MCO 1210.9: SUPPLEMENTARY MOS (SMOS) PROGRAM AND VOLUNTARY LATERAL MOVE PROGRAM FOR MARINE OFFICERS (PCN: 10200790300)
Establishes lateral move and career broadening tour programs for Marine officers.

MCO 1220.5: ENLISTED LATERAL MOVEMENT (PCN: 10200800000)
Establishes procedures for the Marine Corps enlisted lateral movement program.

MCO 1300.8: MARINE CORPS PERSONNEL ASSIGNMENT POLICY
(PCN: 10200820000)
Implements Department of Defense policy and provides guidance relative to the assignment and permanent change of station (PCS) of Marines.

ENCLOSURE (1)

MCO 1300.31: ENLISTED CLASSIFICATION AND ASSIGNMENT DOCUMENTS
(PCN: 10200950100)
Provides field commands with information concerning enlisted personnel status as reflected in the MCTFS.

MCO 1306.16: CONSCIENTIOUS OBJECTORS (PCN: 10201030000)
Provides policy and procedures concerning conscientious objection applicable to all Marines.

MCO 1320.11: PERSONNEL SPONSORSHIP PROGRAM (PCN: 10201080000)
Provides instructions and specific administrative guidance for the conduct of the Marine Corps Personnel Sponsorship Program.

MCO 1326.5: AUTOMATED ORDER WRITING PROCESS (AOWP) (PCN: 10201100300)
Issues instructions regarding promulgation of PCS orders through MCTFS.

MCO P1326.6: SELECTING, SCREENING AND PREPARING ENLISTED MARINES FOR SPECIAL DUTY ASSISNMENTS AND INDEPENDENT DUTIES (SDAMAN)
(PCN: 10201100400)
Provides criteria and assignment prerequisites for the selection of personnel for duty with Marine Corps Security Forces, the Department of State Security Guard Program, and for drill instructor, recruiter, and independent duty assignments.

MCO P1400.31: MARINE CORPS PROMOTION MANUAL, VOLUME 1, OFFICER PROMOTIONS (MARCORPROMMAN, VOL 1, OFFPROM) (PCN: 10201150100)
Contains the basic instructions relative to the administration of officer promotions in the Marine Corps.

MCO P1400.32: MARINE CORPS PROMOTION MANUAL, VOLUME 2, ENLISTED PROMOTIONS (MARCORPROMMAN, VOL 2, ENLPROM) (PCN: 10201150200)
Contains the basic instructions relative to the administration of enlisted promotions in the Marine Corps.

MCO 1510.53: INDIVIDUAL TRAINING STANDARDS (ITS) SYSTEM FOR PERSONNEL AND ADMINISTRATION OCCUPATION FIELD (OCCFLD) 01 (PCN: 10201653500)
Contains ITS for the 01 OccFld.

MCO 1550.26: POLICIES AND PROCEDURES GOVERNING MARINE CORPS INSTITUTE (MCI) TRAINING AND EDUCATION PRODUCT DEVELOPMENT (PCN: 10201901000)
Sets forth service record entry requirements upon course completion, failure, disenrollment, and transfer.

MCO 1560.15: MARINE CORPS ENLISTED COMMISSIONING EDUCATION PROGRAM (MECEP) (PCN: 10201950000)
Provides instructions pertaining to applications for and administration of the MECEP.

ENCLOSURE (1)

MCO 1560.28: VETERANS' EDUCATIONAL ASSISTANCE BENEFITS
(PCN: 10201991200)
Sets forth policies and procedures governing VA education or assistance available to eligible Marine Corps personnel.

MCO P1610.7: PERFORMANCE EVALUATION SYSTEM (PES) (PCN: 10202100000)
Provides guidance for the administration and operation of the PES for Marine Corps officers and noncommissioned officers and for Navy personnel assigned to Marine Corps commands.

MCO 1610.11: PERFORMANCE EVALUATION APPEALS (PCN: 10202110200)
Provides procedures whereby officers and noncommissioned officers (sergeant and above) may submit fitness report appeals to the Board for Correction of Naval Records (BCNR) via the Performance Evaluation Review Board (PERB).

MCO 1650.19: ADMINISTRATIVE AND ISSUE PROCEDURES FOR DECORATIONS, MEDALS AND AWARDS (PCN: 10202200000)
Prescribes procedures and instructions for issuing decorations, medals and awards and sets forth policy guidance for award recommendations.

MCO 1700.22: ALCOHOLIC BEVERAGE CONTROL IN THE MARINE CORPS
(PCN: 10202320100)
Publishes Marine Corps policy concerning the possession, consumption, and sale of alcoholic beverages within the Marine Corps. This order requires the commander to publish detailed alcoholic beverage control instructions.

MCO 1700.23: REQUEST MAST (PCN: 10202320200)
Sets forth Marine Corps request mast policy and procedures.

MCO 1740.13: FAMILY CARE PLANS (PCN: 10202426000)
Publishes policy and establishes procedures for child care plans for dual-service parents and all single parents having custody of their children.

MCO P1741.8: GOVERNMENT LIFE INSURANCE MANUAL (PCN: 10202440000)
Publishes information and establishes standing operating procedures for the administration of Servicemen's Group Life Insurance (SGLI), Veterans Group Life Insurance (VGLI), National Service Life Insurance (NSLI), and the United States Government Life Insurance (USGLI) within the Marine Corps.

MCO P1741.11: SURVIVOR BENEFIT PLAN (SBP) (PCN: 10202460100)
Publishes policies and procedures for the implementation and administration of the SBP.

ENCLOSURE (1)

MCO P1751.3: BASIC ALLOWANCE FOR QUARTERS (BAQ) FOR MARINES WITH DEPENDENTS (PCN: 10202550000)
Provides instructions for the administration of applications for BAQ for Marines (both officers and enlisted) with dependents and related matters.

MCO P1754.4: EXCEPTIONAL FAMILY MEMBER PROGRAM (EFMP SOP) (PCN: 10202565300)
Provides guidance to assign eligible members to EFMP.

MCO 1770.2: NOTICE OF ELIGIBILITY (NOE) BENEFITS FOR MEMBERS OF THE MARINE CORPS RESERVE (PCN: 10202657000)
Provides instructions concerning the administration of the NOE Program, to include the processing of NOE packages for reservists injured on inactive duty or active duty for 30 days or less.

MCO P1900.16: MARINE CORPS SEPARATION AND RETIREMENT MANUAL (MARCORSEPMAN) (PCN: 10202730000)
Establishes instructions, regulations, and policies on separations and retirements.

MCO P3000.15: MANPOWER UNIT DEPLOYMENT PROGRAM STANDING OPERATING PROCEDURES (MANPOWER UDP SOP) (PCN: 10203045500)
Establishes policies and procedures for deployment of units in connection with the UDP.

MCO P3040.4: MARINE CORPS CASUALTY PROCEDURES MANUAL (MARCORCASPROCMAN) (PCN: 10203060000)
Provides guidance for all personnel responsible for Marine Corps casualty reporting, notification assistance, and casualty follow up matters.

MCO 3574.2: ENTRY LEVEL AND SUSTAINMENT LEVEL MARKSMANSHIP TRAINING WITH THE M16A2 SERVICE RIFLE AND M9 SERVICE PISTOL (PCN: 10203380000)
Establishes Marine Corps policy and prescribes requirements concerning marksmanship training with individual small arms.

MCO P4050.38: PERSONAL EFFECTS AND BAGGAGE MANUAL (PCN: 10204190000)
Publishes policies and procedures for the administration and disposition of personal effects and baggage.

MCO 4420.4: DEPARTMENT OF DEFENSE ACTIVITY ADDRESS DIRECTORY (DODAAD) (PCN: 10205410000)
Provides amplifying instructions regarding assignment and use of DoD activity address codes.

ENCLOSURE (1)

MCO 4650.30: PORT CALL PROCEDURES APPLICABLE TO THE MOVEMENT OF MARINE CORPS-SPONSORED PASSENGER TRAFFIC BETWEEN CONUS AND OVERSEAS AREAS (INCLUDING ALASKA AND HAWAII) AND WITHIN AND BETWEEN OVERSEAS AREAS (PCN: 10206400000)
Establishes procedures for obtaining transportation arrangements or authority to procure commercial transportation through local carrier agents for Marine Corps-sponsored passenger traffic proceeding between CONUS and overseas areas (including Alaska and Hawaii) and within and between overseas areas.

MCO P4650.37: MARINE CORPS TRAVEL INSTRUCTIONS MANUAL (MCTIM) (PCN: 10206420400)
Provides guidance to Marine Corps commanding officers and disbursing officers in matters pertaining to travel of personnel.

MCO 5000.12: MARINE CORPS POLICY AND PROCEDURES ON PREGNANCY AND PARENTHOOD (PCN: 10207020800)
Establishes Marine Corps policy and procedures concerning retention, assignment, and separation of pregnant Marines.

MCO P5000.14: MARINE CORPS ADMINISTRATIVE PROCEDURES (MCAP) (PCN: 10207021000)
Provides guidance to all commanders and personnel concerned with the operation of staff level, consolidated and individual reporting unit levels administration.

MCO 5040.6: MARINE CORPS INSPECTIONS (PCN: 10207050300)
Sets forth the philosophy and responsibilities for the conduct of inspections, investigations, request mast and oversight of selected programs by the Inspector General of the Marine Corps (IGMC) and designated Marine Corps activities.

MCO P5110.4: THE MARINE CORPS OFFICIAL MAIL PROGRAM (PCN: 10207290300)
Provides information and direction concerning the requirements for using U.S. Marine Corps official mail.

MCO P5110.6: STANDING OPERATING PROCEDURES FOR MARINE CORPS UNIT MAILROOMS (PCN: 10207290500)
Provides instructions concerning the operation of Marine Corps unit mailrooms.

MCO 5210.11: RECORDS MANAGEMENT PROGRAM FOR THE MARINE CORPS (PCN: 10207480000)
States the objectives of the records management program for the Marine Corps and responsibilities for administration.

MCO P5211.2: THE PRIVACY ACT OF 1974 (PCN: 10207495000)
Outlines the policies and procedures governing the collection, safeguarding, maintenance, public notice, use, access, amendment, and dissemination of personal information in systems of records maintained by the Marine Corps.

MCO 5213.7: MARINE CORPS FORMS MANAGEMENT PROGRAM (PCN: 10207530000)
Prescribes policy, procedures, and guidance for the management and control of forms.

MCO 5214.2: MARINE CORPS INFORMATION REQUIREMENTS (REPORTS) MANAGEMENT PROGRAM (PCN: 10207550500)
Prescribes policy, assigns responsibilities, and sets forth guidance for the management and control of information requirements (reports).

MCO P5215.17: THE MARINE CORPS TECHNICAL PUBLICATIONS SYSTEM
(PCN: 10207590200)
Publishes the policies and standards for the operation and maintenance of the Marine Corps Technical Publications System.

MCO 5216.9: HQMC ORGANIZATION AND ORGANIZATION CODES
(PCN: 10207610000)
Provides current information on the HQMC organization and directs the use of HQMC organization codes on communications from and to the Marine Corps.

MCO 5216.16: PROPER USE OF THE TERMS REFERENCE AND ENCLOSURE
(PCN: 10207630800)
Sets forth guidance for the proper use of the terms reference and enclosure when preparing correspondence or directives.

MCO 5216.19: ADMINISTRATIVE ACTION (AA) FORM, NAVMC 10274 (REV. 3-86)
(PCN: 10207631000)
Provides information and instructions for preparation and use of the AA Form.

MCO 5311.1: TOTAL FORCE STRUCTURE PROCESS (TFSP) (PCN: 10207823500)
Publishes policy and guidance for use in establishing manpower requirements and constructing and submitting changes to the Tables of Organization (T/O).

MCO 5512.4: NO-FEE PASSPORTS (PCN: 10208550000)
Provides Marine Corps policy and instructions concerning no-fee passports for Marine Corps-sponsored personnel performing permanent change of station or temporary additional duty (PCS or TAD) travel and the administration of the Marine Corps Passport and Visa Program.

ENCLOSURE (1)

MCO P5512.11: IDENTIFICATION CARDS FOR MEMBERS OF THE UNIFORM SERVICES, THEIR DEPENDENTS, AND OTHER INDIVIDUALS (PCN: 10208570300)
Outlines the regulations and policies for the application, verification, and issuance of identification cards and procedures for Defense Enrollment Eligibility Reporting System (DEERS).

MCO 5600.20: MARINE CORPS WARFIGHTING PUBLICATIONS SYSTEM (PCN: 10208640000)
Provides processes for the development, review, and maintenance processes for warfighting publications.

MCO P5600.31: MARINE CORPS PUBLICATIONS AND PRINTING REGULATIONS (PCN: 10208650000)
Provides policy, regulations, responsibilities, and guidance governing printing and publications.

MCO P5750.1: MANUAL FOR THE MARINE CORPS HISTORICAL PROGRAM (PCN: 10209090000)
Sets forth policies and procedures governing the administration of the Marine Corps Historical Program and delineates the respective responsibilities of Headquarters Marine Corps and field commands in the execution of this program.

MCO P5800.16: MARINE CORPS MANUAL FOR LEGAL ADMINISTRATION (LEGADMINMAN) (PCN: 10209190800)
Publishes policies, procedures, guidance, and instructions for administration actions in implementing the Uniform Code of Military Justice (UCMJ); the Manual for Courts-Martial, 1984 (MCM, 1984); and, the Manual of the Judge Advocate General (JAGMAN).

MCO P6100.12: MARINE CORPS PHYSICAL FITNESS TEST AND BODY COMPOSITION PROGRAM MANUAL (MCPFTBCP) (PCN: 10209350400)
Publishes policy and implementing instructions concerning physical fitness and body composition in the Marine Corps.

MCO 6320.2: ADMINISTRATION AND PROCESSING OF HOSPITALIZED MARINES (PCN: 10209510000)
Publishes instructions for providing prompt and complete administrative assistance to Marines who are hospitalized.

MCO 7130.1: ISSUANCE/MODIFICATION OF PERMANENT CHANGE OF STATION (PCS) TRAVEL ORDERS BY FIELD COMMANDS (PCN: 10209770000)
Delegates' authority to certain field commands for issuance and/or modification of PCS orders and prescribes instructions that will enable HQMC to properly administer the PCS budget.

ENCLOSURE (1)

MCO 7220.12: SPECIAL DUTY ASSIGNMENT (SDA) PAY PROGRAM
(PCN: 10209800000)
Provides instructions for the Special Duty Assignment Pay Program
established by 37 U.S.C. 307.

**MCO 7220.21: POLICY FOR ADVANCE PAY INCIDENT TO A PERMANENT CHANGE OF
STATION (PCS)** (PCN: 10209830000)
Establishes policy with regard to authorizing advance pay for enlisted
members on PCS orders in all pay grades.

MCO 7220.24: SELECTIVE REENLISTMENT BONUS (SRB) PROGRAM
(PCN: 10209860200)
Provides instructions for the administration of the SRB Program authorized
by 37 U.S.C. 308.

MCO 7220.52: FOREIGN LANGUAGE PROFICIENCY PAY (FLPP) PROGRAM
(PCN: 10209913700)
Establishes criteria for designating personnel eligible for and provides
instructions for the administration of the FLPP.

**MCO P7301.104: ACCOUNTING UNDER THE APPROPRIATIONS "MILITARY PERSONNEL,
MARINE CORPS" AND "RESERVE PERSONNEL, MARINE CORPS"** (PCN: 10210256500)

C-9

Publishes detailed accounting data for utilization in accounting for
obligations and expenditures. Use this Manual when formulating travel
appropriation for inclusion in funded travel orders.

MCO 10110.47: BASIC ALLOWANCE FOR SUBSISTENCE (BAS) (PCN: 10210861700)
Outlines the regulations for administration of BAS and procedures for the
issue and control of the Meal Card (DD Form 714).

MCO P10120.28: INDIVIDUAL CLOTHING REGULATIONS (ICR)
(PCN: 10210880000)
Provides current instructions and guidance concerning the administration
of individual uniform clothing.

NAVMC 2922: UNITED STATES MARINE CORPS UNIT AWARDS MANUAL
(PCN: 10001361200)
Lists all unit awards that have been presented to Marine Corps units since
the beginning of World War II.

NAVSO P-6034: JOINT FEDERAL TRAVEL REGULATIONS (JFTR), VOLUME 1
(PCN: 20360340000)
Contains basic statutory regulations concerning travel and transportation
allowance of members of the uniformed services, including all Regular and
Reserve components thereof.

ENCLOSURE (1)

NTP-3: TELECOMMUNICATIONS USERS MANUAL (PCN: 50100378000)
Establishes the current message preparation procedures for both military
and commercial addressees.

**NTP 3 SUPP 1: U.S. NAVY ADDRESS INDICATING GROUP (AIG) AND COLLECTIVE
ADDRESS DESIGNATOR (CAD) HANDBOOK** (PCN: 50100379000)
Contains instructions for the use of AIGs; a numerical list of AIGs,
cognizant authority and purpose; a numerical listing and composition of
unique AIGs; instructions for the use of CADs; and, an alphabetical list
of authorized CADs with cognizant authority and purpose.

SECNAVINST 1650.1: NAVY MARINE CORPS AWARDS MANUAL (PCN: 21600050000)
Contains administrative procedures, information and regulations concerning
current awards available to individuals and units in the naval service.

**SECNAVINST 5210.11: DEPARTMENT OF THE NAVY FILE MAINTENANCE PROCEDURES
AND STANDARD SUBJECT IDENTIFICATION CODES (SSIC)** (PCN: 21600280000)
Outlines the process for segregating and filing Navy and Marine Corps
records and acts as the single standard system of numbers and/or letter
symbols used throughout the Department of the Navy for: categorizing and
subject classifying Navy and Marine Corps
information; identifying directives, blank forms, and reports; and
establishing filing and retrieval systems.

SECNAVINST 5212.5: NAVY AND MARINE CORPS RECORDS DISPOSITION MANUAL
(PCN: 21600355600)
Prescribes policy and procedures for the maintenance, use, and disposition
of naval records.

SECNAVINST 5215.1: DEPARTMENT OF THE NAVY DIRECTIVES ISSUANCE SYSTEM
Contains policies, responsibilities, and standards for the administration
of the Department of the Navy Directives Issuance System.

SECNAVINST 5216.5: DEPARTMENT OF THE NAVY CORRESPONDENCE MANUAL
(PCN: 21600400000)
Prescribes policies, procedures, and guidance for the preparation of
correspondence.

UDS-1080-02: UNIT DIARY SYSTEM (UDS) USER'S MANUAL (PCN: 18710800200)
Provides a source document for training and operation for all UDS users.

UM-OLDS: USER'S MANUAL (UM) FOR THE ON-LINE DIARY SYSTEM (OLDS)
(PCN: 10000001500)
Provides detailed instructions and procedures for using the OLDS.

USN PLAD 1: MESSAGE ADDRESS DIRECTORY (PCN: 50100379100)
This joint services publication contains a standard listing of all Army,
Air Force, Navy, Marine Corps, and Coast Guard plain language address
designators, plus joint service/DoD plain language addresses used in the
preparation of messages.

U.S. NAVY REGULATIONS (PCN: 50100370000)
Contains chapters setting forth authority and responsibilities of the
Commandant of the Marine Corps, commanding officers, and other commanders;
precedence, authority and command; honors and ceremonies, etc.

ENCLOSURE (1)

INDIVIDUALS MARINES' ADMINISTRATIVE RESPONSIBILITIES

Commanders are ultimately responsible for the accuracy of their Marines' records. However, individual Marines are also responsible for the accuracy of their records, especially information for which they are the source. Specific individual responsibilities include:

1. Reviewing Service Record Books and Officer Qualification Records. These documents are typically formally audited every time a Marine is transferred, and at other times as determined by command and Marine Corps policy. Marines, assisted by their commander and the IPAC as necessary, should take immediate action to correct any errors identified during these reviews.

2. Reviewing the accuracy of information in MCTFS via Marine OnLine (https://www.mol.usmc.mil). Certain information, such as addresses, phone numbers, and religion, can be input by the individual Marine. Changes to more sensitive information must be submitted with supporting documentation to the command or supporting IPAC.

3. Ensuring documents are accurate and up-to-date; e.g., marriage documents, divorce documents, family member documentation, Exceptional Family Member Program documentation, etc.

4. Properly requesting, checking out on, and checking in from leave.

5. Ensuring Record of Emergency Data (RED), Servicemen's Group Life Insurance (SGLI), Basic Training Record (BTR), and Basic Individual Record (BIR) are accurate and that any changes are submitted in a timely manner.

6. Submitting documents relating to special qualifications such as jump records and school certificates.

7. Reviewing Leave & Earnings Statement (LES) and notifying the commander of any errors. MyPay (https://mypay.dfas.mil/) is the primary method for reviewing LESs and changing selected financial information.

8. Ensuring all orders and related claims documents are accurate.

9. Reporting any changes or discrepancies in pay and benefits.

10. Reporting changes to their medical status.

11. Ensuring, via Marine OnLine, the accuracy of their career service dates including Pay Entry Base Date (PEBD), retirement date, Armed Forces Active Duty Base Date (AFADBD), Date Entered Armed Forces (DEAF)

ENCLOSURE (2)

12. Periodically reviewing their Official Military Personnel File (OMPF) and Master Brief Sheet (MBS).

13. Ensuring all information in the Defense Enrollment Eligibility Reporting System (DEERS) is accurate and up-to-date by either contacting their local RAPIDS/military ID card facility or by calling 1(800) 538-9552.

ENCLOSURE (2)

COMMANDERS' RESPONSIBILITIES FOR PERSONNEL ADMINISTRATION

1. Commanders are responsible for the accuracy of their Marines' military records, regardless of the format of the information (paper records, MCTFS records, etc.) and the location of the records (mainframe databases, IPAC, etc.). Much of the information previously reported at personnel administration centers can now be reported and reviewed by the commander and
the individual Marine via Marine Online. More complex information requirements and process will be facilitated by
the supporting IPAC.

2. Commanders are specifically responsible for the following:

    a. Establishing command procedures for receiving IPAC support and ensuring connectivity with the IPAC. For administration to function efficiently, free and open exchange of information must exist between the unit and the IPAC.

    b. Submitting accurate Unit Management Status Reports via Marine OnLine.

    c. Submitting training information.

    d. Submitting Proficiency and Conduct Marks (Pro/Con).

    e. Recommending/not recommending Marines for promotion.

    f. Recommending/not recommending Marines for reenlistment.

    g. Recommending and approving Marines for awards.

    h. Ensuring their Marines are provided access to Marine OnLine and MyPay

    i. Managing leave and special liberty.

    j. Submitting completed Unit Punishment Book (UPB) forms, to include results of trial by courts-martial, to the supporting IPAC.

    k. Counseling and authenticating administrative remarks entries (Page 11) in the Service Record Book (SRB) and Officer Qualification Record (OQR).

l. Forwarding limited-duty documents to the IPAC.

m. Processing administrative discharges.

n. Reporting accurate unit Personnel Tempo (PersTempo), Deployment Tempo (DepTempo), and Operational Tempo (OpTempo).

o. Reporting changes of individual personnel status to the IPAC.

p. Complying with Physical Evaluation Board (PEB) tracking and administration and ensuring appropriate documents are forwarded to the supporting IPAC.

q. Maintaining an effective meal card management program. (Note: Meal cards are issued and retrieved at the PACs - commanders need to retrieve them temporarily from Marines going TAD or on leave.)

r. Processing fitness reports.

s. Reviewing the command payroll and reporting discrepancies to the IPAC.

ENCLOSURE (3)

RESPONSIBILITIES OF G-1S, S-1S, AND ADMINISTRATIVE OFFICERS

1. Every Marine Corps command requires administrative support and oversight. At the Major Subordinate Command level and above, these responsibilities are usually located in a G-1 section. Regiments, Groups, Battalions and Squadrons usually have an S-1 section to perform these functions. The size and makeup of these sections will vary according to the size, mission, and location of the organization.

2. Following is a list of command responsibilities that are typically carried out by G-1 and S-1 sections. Individuals in commands and sections that do not have dedicated G-1 or S-1 sections also carry many of these responsibilities, for example, the Company First Sergeant may be assigned responsibility for his company's career management and retention programs.

3. Where applicable, these responsibilities apply to all personnel assigned to or supported by the command, including Marines, civilians, and other service personnel. **This list is guidance only and in no way limits a commander's flexibility to assign responsibilities in the manner that best supports his command's mission.**

   a. Administrative support to the command

   b. Coordinate internal and external administrative requirements.

   c. Track and monitor urgent administrative support requested by higher headquarters and/or subordinate commands.

   d. Prepare and publish duty roster assignments.

   e. Plan, organize, and monitor protocol and ceremonial functions.

   f. Publish staff regulations.

   g. Maintain appropriate portions of the Command Readiness Brief.

   h. Prepare, review and staff command correspondence.

   i. Coordinate the command's Equal Employment Opportunity (EEO) Program.

   j. Manage the commands' performance evaluations program.

   k. Process personal, unit, and special awards.

   l. Manage the Casualty Affairs Program.

m. Manage the command mail/postal program.

n. Manage limited-duty documentation.

o. Maintain command files.

p. Manage the acquisition, distribution control, and accountability of the command's publications and manage the Directive Control Point (DCP).

q. Manage the command's forms management.

r. Monitor the receipt and delivery of promotion warrants.

s. Assist the commander with completing promotion recommendations and non-recommendations.

t. Manage and coordinate, and monitor the information flow between the command and the supporting IPAC.

u. Manage the command's procedures for Personnel Action Requests (PARs). A PAR requests resolution on any administrative problem and is submitted via the chain of command. PARs that cannot be resolved within the command may be routed to the supporting IPAC for resolution.

4. Manpower functions

a. Manage the command's Manpower resources. Track, monitor, and distribute manpower assets to ensure the command and subordinate units are appropriately staffed.

b. Make personnel assignments and monitor the command's human resources.

c. Review, coordinate, and provide guidance on all Tables of Organization and Equipment issues

d. Submit personnel statistic data for the command's Status of Resources and Training Systems (SORTS) reporting.

e. Issue command special orders.

f. Manage command staffing slates.

g. Submit strength reports to higher headquarters.

h.   Prepare, endorse, and distribute Permanent Change of Station, Permanent Change of Assignment, and command special orders.

i.   Manage the command's Individual Mobilization Augmentees (IMA) program.

5.   Operational responsibilities

a.   Recommending to the commander the required administrative and personnel resources to meet operational requirements.

b.   Identify, source, and coordinate augmentation requirements and assignments.

c.   Calculate casualty estimations.

d.   Develop, draft, and approve OPLAN/Annex E with Appendices.

e.   Publish Joint and Combined Personnel Status Reports.

f.   Participate as required in Operational Planning Teams (OPT) and provide appropriate estimates of supportability

g.   Provide representation to the Command Center, Combat Operations Center, etc.

h.   Provide Tactical Exercise Employment Program (TEEP) planning, input, and personnel statistical data.

i.   Develop and publishes the command's Tactical Standard Operational Procedures.

j.   Manage reserve augmentation and mobilization policy and requirements.

6.   Career planning and retention

a.   Manage the command's First-Term Alignment Plan (FTAP) and Subsequent-Term Alignment Plan (STAP) Programs.

b.   Manage the command's career counseling program; advise commanders and Marines of career progression tracks and professional development for all assigned personnel, to include, counseling Marines on all available enlisted to officer programs.

c.   Manage and coordinate special assignment compliance and screening requirements.

    d. Manage and supervise the command's Transitional Assistance Program/Transitional Assistance Management Program (TAP/TAMP).

    e. Manage the Marine-for-Life Program.

    f. Manage the Survivor Benefit Program (SBP).

7. Legal

    a. Manage command legal matters.

    b. Prepare Unit Punishments Book (UPBs). Coordinate with supporting IPAC as required.

    c. Prepare and provide a complete summary transcript of proceedings for all Non-Judicial Punishment (NJP) administered within the command.

    d. Account for and report absentees and deserters, to include the preparation of DD Form 553 and DD Form 616.

    e. Prepare documents to effect reductions in grade.

    f. Provide administrative support on all matters of investigation and formal inquiries. This includes the execution of JAG Manual Investigations, Line of Duty Investigations, and Preliminary Inquiries.

    g. Provide required legal support within the organization; such as, coordination for the completion of wills/power of attorney and chaser assignments.

    h. Process administrative separations.

    i. Prepare and submit appellate leave packages to the servicing Staff Judge Advocate with a copy to the servicing IPAC.

    j. Perform notary public responsibilities.

8. Civilian personnel

    a. Manage, civilian personnel staffing, advancements, position description reviews, and job announcements.

    b. Coordinate civilian personnel labor relations.

    c. Coordinate, as necessary, with the supporting Human Resource Office (HRO).

ENCLOSURE (4)

9. Information security

    a. Manage the CMCC and coordinate access to classified information with the security manager.

    b. Assist with managing the command's Information and Personnel Security Program.

    c. Manage the command's Freedom of Information Act (FOIA).

    d. Manage the command's Privacy Act program.

    e. Manage the command's Unit Information Program.

10. Marine and family services, personal readiness and community support

    a. Serve as the command's liaison to the Marine Corps Community Services (MCCS) for family readiness.

    b. Manage the Command's Family Readiness Programs, including the Family Advocacy Program, the Key Volunteer Network (KVN) Program, and the Exceptional Family Member Program (EMFP).

    c. Manage personal support programs including the Semper Fit Program, the Education Program, Exchange and Club services, the Recreation Program, Fundraising and Navy Relief Drives, and the Substance Abuse Control Programs.

    d. Manage programs that support families of deployed personnel.

INSTALLATION PERSONNEL ADMINISTRATION CENTERS RESPONSIBILITIES

1. Installation Personnel Administration Centers (IPACs) support commands and individual Marines in a defined geographic area. In order to provide prompt and accurate personnel administrative support, the following areas are provided as guidance for IPACs and supported commands. This guidance is based on lessons learned from numerous configurations of consolidated administration. **Each IPAC's specific functions, organization, and support relationships will be tailored to the supported commands' mission requirements.**

2. Command support and customer service

    a. Establish procedures for providing for receiving, monitoring, and completing, requests for assistance from supported commanders and Marines.

    b. Provide supported commands access to Service Record Books and Officer Qualification Records and assist commands with obtaining information and reports from manpower information systems.

    c. Provide necessary support to unit reporting of legal administrative matters, to include Non-Judicial Punishment and Courts-Martial.

    d. Identify and track those Marines assigned to a limited-duty status. Process limited-duty documentation, report appropriate duty status and limitation codes, and monitor re-evaluation timelines and deadlines.

    e. Establish Meal Card issue and recovery procedures. Particular attention must be made to appointment letters, required logbook entries, inventory requirements, and accountability.

    f. Assist commanders, as necessary, with obtaining administrative support beyond the IPAC's capabilities.

3. Pay

    a. Assist commands with tracking and monitoring pay-related issues.

    b. Monitor "Update and Extract Cycles" for Inconsistent Conditions, Suspect Payments, Direct Deposit participation, and ensures corrective action is completed prior to the upcoming payday as required.

    c. Process requests for special payments, liquidations, waivers or remissions of indebtedness.

ENCLOSURE (5)

4. Joins

    a. Endorse and/or receive PCS/PCA/TAD orders with endorsements from supported commands. All inbound personnel must have a reporting endorsement for PCS orders prior to reporting the join entry or submitting a travel claim for settlement. Orders endorsement may be from the IPAC or the supported command.

    b. Process advance pay requests from newly joined Marines.

    c. Process station allowances. Written internal control procedures should be established to identify external relationships with local housing directors.

    d. Report Basic Allowance for Housing (BAH)/Overseas Housing Allowance (OHA).

    e. Complete join audits through a personal interview with the individual Marine upon reporting to the command; report all necessary information updates.

    f. Complete the second stage audit after elapsed time has posted or 60 days after the join entry has processed, whichever is earlier.

    g. Identify inbound personnel promoted en route for appropriate action.

    h. Identify appropriate payments, credits, and checkages for special pay, hazardous duty pay, hardship duty pay, and combat zone tax exclusions.

    i. Complete travel claims and submit them to the servicing Finance Officer. IPAC procedures must include tracking of the PCS travel claim from the individual Marine's submission of the claim at the IPAC, forwarding to
the servicing Finance Officer and delivery of the settled claim to the individual Marine.

5. Orders

    a. Prepare, endorse, and deliver Temporary Additional Duty, Permanent Change of Station, Permanent Change of Assignment, reserve, and separation orders. Ensures appropriate record entries are accomplished.

    b. Prepare, submit, and track submission of travel claims for permanent and temporary duty travel.

ENCLOSURE (5)

2

c. Notify Marines and commands of orders received at IPAC.

d. Ensure members have sufficient obligated service for orders execution.

e. Request port-call.

f. Request area clearances.

g. Apply for no-fee passports.

h. Submit for travel advances.

i. Assist command representatives with required special duty screenings.

j. Process reserve In-Progress Payments (IPP).

k. Processing separations and retirements.

6. Deployments

a. Assist commanders with determining and requesting deployed administrative support. Considerations include personnel augmentation, reach-back procedures, and system/connectivity requirements.

b. Provide required reach-back support capabilities for deployed units.

c. Assist commands with completing deployment record book audits and reporting of deployment-related information. Pay particular attention to entitlements authorized in conjunction with the deployment including Hostile Fire Pay, Family Separation Allowance, career sea pay, combat zone tax exclusion, and reserve carried forward leave balance.

d. Provide pre-deployment training for unit administrative personnel.

7. Quality control

a. Develop internal controls that ensure quality assurance and timely reporting.

b. Establish internal controls to ensure compliance with current directives and accurate reporting.

ENCLOSURE (5)

c. Provide advice to commanders for compliance with Marine Corps, Department of the Navy, and Department of Defense policies, plans and regulations.

d. Assist commands with completing required record audits.

e. Manage feedback reports and make all required corrective actions or entries.

REPONSIBILITIES OF THE MANPOWER INFORMATION SYSTEMS SUPPORT OFFICE

1. MISSOs are agencies of Headquarters Marine Corps Manpower and Reserve Affairs Department, Manpower Information System Support Division (MI). The MISSO's responsibilities include:

    a. Providing support and training for manpower information systems.

    b. Establishing unit access to manpower information systems.

    c. Assisting commanders and IPACs with determining deployed systems requirements.

    d. Receiving, reviewing, and submitting trouble calls beyond the MISSO's capabilities to the Manpower Information Systems Support Activity.